Original title:
Unbroken Dreams

Copyright © 2025 Swan Charm
All rights reserved.

Author: Olivia Oja
ISBN HARDBACK: 978-9908-1-4576-1
ISBN PAPERBACK: 978-9908-1-4577-8
ISBN EBOOK: 978-9908-1-4578-5

A Tapestry Woven with Stardust

In the night sky, wishes gleam,
A dance of dreams, a silent theme.
Threads of silver, whispered light,
Weaving stories, taking flight.

Each twinkling star, a tale untold,
In cosmic arms, the brave and bold.
Moments caught in timeless grace,
A tapestry, our souls embrace.

Fragments of a Daring Heart

Shattered pieces lie on the floor,
Each one whispers of battles and war.
A heart once whole, now bravely scarred,
In fragments lies a spirit marred.

Yet through the cracks, light starts to seep,
With every breath, promises keep.
Daring journeys wait ahead,
For hearts reborn from ashes spread.

The Light Beyond the Shadowed Path

In shadows deep, a flicker gleams,
A guiding light, the heart still dreams.
Through twisted turns and winding ways,
Hope ignites the darkest days.

With every step, courage grows strong,
Leading us where we belong.
The dawn will break, the night will fade,
In light's embrace, our fears invade.

Threads of Aspirations Unraveled

A tapestry frayed at the seams,
Woven with hopes and whispered dreams.
Each thread pulled tight, then let go,
Reveals the paths we dare to sow.

Yet in the unraveling, we find,
The beauty of being unconfined.
For in the loose ends lies our art,
A vibrant dance of the human heart.

A Journey Reimagined

In whispers soft the path unwinds,
Through forests deep where clarity finds.
With every step the heart beats bold,
As stories of old begin to unfold.

Mountains rise with grandeur high,
Underneath the ever-changing sky.
Each moment lingers, breath held tight,
A dance of shadows in fading light.

Rivers carve their tales in stone,
Flowing freely, they sing alone.
With every twist, new sights appear,
A symphony of dreams drawing near.

Fading footprints mark the trail,
Tales of wonder in every gale.
Echoes of laughter weave through the trees,
In the hush of nature, a gentle breeze.

As dawn breaks forth with blush and light,
Hope awakens, dispelling the night.
The journey continues, forever anew,
With each step I take, the world feels true.

Embrace of the Sky

In twilight's glow where dreams take flight,
Stars awaken in the cloak of night.
A canvas vast, painted with grace,
Inviting all to find their place.

Clouds like whispers drift and sway,
Carrying secrets of the day.
Their shadows dance on the fields below,
In this embrace, time moves slow.

Beneath the moon, the world sleeps tight,
Wrapped in a blanket of silver light.
But hearts awaken, spirits soar,
In the embrace of the sky, we explore.

Winds of change bring life anew,
As colors blend, a vibrant hue.
With every breath, the cosmos calls,
In this vastness, our spirit sprawls.

So lift your gaze, let worries cease,
In the embrace of the sky, find peace.
For in this heaven, we are free,
Boundless souls, in destiny.

Rise from the Ashes

From the depths of despair, we rise,
With embers of hope in our eyes.
Each scar tells a story of fight,
As we step into the warm light.

With courage, we shatter the chains,
Transforming our losses to gains.
The ashes that whispered our fears,
Now fuel the fire of our years.

We dance with the winds of change,
Embracing the power to rearrange.
From ruins, a strength is reborn,
A phoenix that greets the dawn.

No longer defined by the past,
Our spirits soar, bold and steadfast.
Together we stand, hand in hand,
Building anew on this land.

The journey continues, we vow,
In unity, we flourish, somehow.
For from the ashes, we have soared,
In resilience, our hearts are restored.

Bridges of Resilience

Across the river of doubt we tread,
Building bridges with words unsaid.
With every step, we break the mold,
Turning dreams into stories bold.

In the storms, we learn to bend,
Strength found in every loyal friend.
Together, we weather the night,
Carving paths in the fading light.

Each struggle is a stone we lay,
Forging a route to brighter days.
With hearts anchored, we take the leap,
A promise to never lose sleep.

In the shadows, we find our way,
Creating hope where we may stray.
These bridges of resilience stand tall,
Welcoming each rise and each fall.

Though challenges test our resolve,
In unity, our doubts dissolve.
We rise together, side by side,
In the power of love, we abide.

Illuminating the Unknown

In the silence, whispers begin,
A light flickers, inviting within.
Through shadows, we bravely approach,
To find paths that fear cannot broach.

Each question a spark in the night,
Guiding us towards wisdom's light.
With every step, the mist clears,
As courage dispels our deepest fears.

Embracing the journey unknown,
In the heart, resilience is grown.
With every lesson that we glean,
The unseen becomes the serene.

We dance with the mysteries wide,
In faith, we keep hope as our guide.
For within the dark, a fire burns,
Illuminating the path that returns.

The thrill of discovery awaits,
Redirecting our fate through the gates.
In the unknown, we find our way,
A journey of light that holds sway.

The Radiance of Daybreak

As dawn's first light breaks the night,
Whispers of hope take flight.
Golden rays embrace the earth,
Heralding the promise of rebirth.

With gentle hues, the world awakes,
Each moment a chance that life takes.
In the silence, dreams converge,
As shadows of yesterday purge.

The symphony of morning sings,
A canvas where new beginnings spring.
In every heart, a spark resides,
A yearning for truth that abides.

With fresh eyes, we greet the day,
Letting love guide our way.
In the warmth of the sun's soft glow,
We find strength in the seeds we sow.

Together we dance in radiant grace,
In the light, there is always a place.
For the dawn holds the promise so dear,
That each day brings us closer, my dear.

Lighthouses in the Fog

In the mist, they stand tall,
Guiding ships through the night.
Their beams cut through shadows,
A promise of safe flight.

Whispers of the sea call,
As waves crash on stone.
Each light a beacon bright,
For sailors all alone.

Flickering hopes arise,
In darkness, we trust.
The lighthouses shine on,
Transforming fear to dust.

Through storms and through calm,
Their strength never wavers.
A silent vow kept tight,
To serve as our saviors.

In every heart they dwell,
Stirring the courage deep.
Lighthouses in the fog,
Guard dreams we dare to keep.

Canvassing Our Aspirations

A brush dipped in hope,
Colors blend and collide.
On canvas, our dreams bloom,
With passion as our guide.

Sketches of future paths,
Lines drawn with intent.
Each stroke, a heart's desire,
And time, we circumvent.

Vivid hues of vision,
Splash against the grey.
In this gallery of wishes,
We paint a brand new day.

From whispers to bold claims,
We strive through the fight.
Creating our own worlds,
Beneath the starlit night.

With every brush in hand,
The canvas comes alive.
Canvassing aspirations,
In art, our dreams survive.

The Bridge of Faith

Across the chasm wide,
A bridge of dreams is built.
Step by step we wander,
Over doubt and guilt.

Each plank a story told,
Of struggles faced before.
With courage as our guide,
We seek and yearn for more.

Beneath the skies so vast,
Our hearts begin to soar.
The bridge connects our hopes,
To realms we can't ignore.

Hand in hand, we traverse,
With faith as our refrain.
In unity, we rise,
Through joy and through pain.

When storms may shake our way,
And visions seem to fade,
The bridge of faith holds strong,
Together, unafraid.

Dreams Like Wildflowers

In fields of golden light,
Wildflowers dance and sway.
Each petal tells a tale,
Of hope along the way.

With colors bright and bold,
They blanket the green ground.
A tapestry of wishes,
In every bloom, they're found.

They bend but do not break,
In winds both fierce and kind.
Nature's gentle whispers,
Guide dreams that are entwined.

Through seasons of despair,
They brave the pouring rain.
Like dreams, they fight to grow,
Emerging once again.

In the sun's warm embrace,
Their fragrance fills the air.
Dreams like wildflowers flourish,
With love, they find their share.

Colors of the Sky

The dawn brings whispers, soft and bright,
Pastels blend, a glorious sight.
Clouds dance gently, on blue's expanse,
Nature's canvas, a vibrant romance.

When sunset glows in fiery red,
Horizons blaze, the day has fled.
Stars emerge, like jewels in the night,
Painting dreams in shimmering light.

The moon takes stage, a silver queen,
Her soft embrace, a tranquil sheen.
Night's cool breath, an ode so deep,
In colors of the sky, secrets sleep.

Unfolding Pages

A book lies waiting, stories untold,
Whispers of journeys, both brave and bold.
Each turning leaf, a new world unfolds,
In ink-stained wisdom, life's truth is scrolled.

Fables of old in shadows reside,
Adventures beckon, with arms open wide.
Characters dance, in laughter and tears,
Pages turn softly, through hopes and fears.

The wisdom of ages, a silent guide,
In every chapter, love does abide.
With every read, new dreams take flight,
Unfolding pages in the dead of night.

Voices of the Unseen

In quiet corners, whispers reside,
Echoes of hearts, where shadows hide.
Gentle beings, not seen, but felt,
In every heartbeat, their magic knelt.

The murmurs of trees in the evening breeze,
Soft voices sing through rustling leaves.
The stories of earth, the tales of the sky,
In silence and shadow, they softly lie.

Each fleeting moment, a chance to hear,
The voices of souls, who linger near.
In every heartbeat, their truths resound,
In this unseen realm, love is profound.

The Journey Within

A winding path, through valleys and peaks,
A voyage of self, where the spirit seeks.
In silence we wander, in thoughts we dive,
The heart is the compass, the soul is alive.

From shadows we learn, from light we grow,
Through the depths of sorrow, and the joy we sow.
Each lesson a bridge, to the answers we find,
In the journey within, we discover the mind.

With every step taken, the layers unveil,
The stories of courage, through trials we sail.
A tapestry woven with dreams and fears,
In the journey within, the truth appears.

The Glitter of Long-Shelved Aspirations

In shadows dreams lay still, waiting,
Time whispers tales of what might be.
In the silence, hope keeps baiting,
A flicker of what could set us free.

Dusty paths of yesteryears,
With echoes of laughter lingering.
The heart remembers all the fears,
Yet still it craves the joy of spring.

Bright glimmers dance in twilight's hue,
Unraveled threads of vibrant schemes.
In the quiet, the soul breaks through,
To reclaim the lost, to chase the dreams.

Adventures once postponed abide,
In the corners of our weary minds.
With every breath, new worlds collide,
Reviving the light that fate unwinds.

So gather dust and chase the gleam,
For time can nurture need and want.
In the tapestry, weave a dream,
For each aspiration has its haunt.

A Radiant Flicker in the Stillness

In the hush before the dawn breaks,
A flicker dances on serene air.
Hope awakens, gently it wakes,
Glowing softly, beyond despair.

Stars whisper secrets in the night,
As darkness cradles fragile beams.
Each spark a promise, pure and bright,
Carried forward in silent dreams.

Beneath the calm, a fire burns low,
Embers of wishes long embraced.
In stillness, hearts begin to glow,
Illuminating every place.

With every breath, the light expands,
Guiding souls through uncharted seas.
In unity, the world understands,
A radiant flicker sets minds at ease.

So cherish the moments, keep them near,
For in silence, truth often sings.
In gleaming whispers, we persevere,
Finding strength in the hope each spark brings.

The Pulse of Forgotten Tomorrows

In the echoes of what could have been,
Lies a pulse beneath the dust of time.
Like waves retreating to begin,
The heart remembers every rhyme.

Dreams deferred in shadows laid,
Yearn for sunlight's warm return.
Their essence cannot be betrayed,
In whispered memories, they burn.

Rivers of promise, deep and vast,
Flow through minds like gentle streams.
Each current pulls us to the past,
Reviving the fervor of lost dreams.

With every heartbeat, we advance,
The rhythm of fate beats strong and true.
In the dance of life's strange chance,
We forge a path anew with hues.

So let the pulse ignite our way,
Embrace the echoes, heed their call.
Together we can seize the day,
And rise from shadows, never fall.

Navigating the Chaos of Everything

In the whirlwind of this endless race,
We search for peace amid the noise.
With every step, we find our place,
And reclaim the beauty where joy deploys.

Fragments fly in wild array,
Yet in the storm, a compass found.
With steady hands, we chart the way,
Through currents fierce and swirling ground.

Amid the chaos, we seek calm,
A steady flame in shifting sand.
With every breath, we find the balm,
To guide our hearts, to make a stand.

The tides of life may pull and sway,
But in the tempest, we will strive.
With courage bright, we'll break the gray,
And carve our paths, each voice alive.

So brace the storm, embrace its call,
For in the chaos, hope can thrive.
Together we shall rise and fall,
Navigating all with hearts alive.

Moonlit Aspirations

Under the silver glow, we dream,
Whispers of night, a gentle stream.
Stars align in the cosmic dance,
Guiding our hearts toward chance.

In shadows deep, we find our light,
Embracing hopes that take their flight.
With every breath, the moon's embrace,
We chase the dreams, we seek our place.

Crickets sing in the cool night air,
Each note a promise, a silent prayer.
With twinkling eyes, we take the leap,
Into the unknown, our secrets keep.

Beneath the sky so vast and wide,
We gather strength, our fears aside.
The moon, our witness, shines so bright,
In the silence, we find our might.

Together we rise, no end in sight,
In moonlit dreams, we find our light.
A journey forged with every breath,
Embodying life, defying death.

The Unyielding Spirit

Through trials faced and battles won,
The spirit shines like the morning sun.
With every scar, a tale unfolds,
Of courage held and dreams retold.

The mountains high, we dare to climb,
With hearts aflame, we bend not time.
Like rivers flow, we find our way,
In the darkest night, we seize the day.

With roots held strong in fertile ground,
In whispered winds, our strength is found.
Through storm and strife, we persevere,
Guardians of hope, we hold it dear.

Every challenge, a chance to grow,
Through ashes rise, like fire's glow.
Together we stand, unbroken, free,
An unyielding spirit, eternally.

With hands uplifted, we touch the sky,
In unity, no bounds apply.
The journey forward, a path to chart,
An anthem of strength, a beating heart.

Seasons of Renewal

Leaves of gold drift on the breeze,
Whispers of change in the old oak trees.
With every spring, we bloom anew,
In the warmth of sunlight, life breaks through.

As winter's chill begins to fade,
Hope rises up, in colors laid.
Daffodils dance in the gentle thaw,
Nature's canvas, a sight to draw.

In summer's glow, we laugh and play,
Chasing daylight throughout the day.
With sunsets painted in hues so bright,
We gather memories, pure delight.

As autumn calls with its crisp air,
We pause to ponder, to reflect and share.
In every season, a lesson learned,
A cycle endless, as life is turned.

Through each transition, we find our grace,
In the dance of time, we find our place.
Embracing change, we rise and stand,
Together united, hand in hand.

The Eye of the Storm

In the tempest's rage, we find our core,
A quiet eye, amidst the roar.
Beneath the chaos, a peace concealed,\nThrough wild winds, our fate revealed.

The clouds may darken, the thunder roll,
Yet deep within, we guard our soul.
With steady hearts, we face the fight,
In darkest hours, we find our light.

As lightning strikes and shadows sway,
We hold our ground, come what may.
With courage bold, we pierce the night,
In unity, we'll shine so bright.

When storms settle, and calm takes hold,
Reflections clear, our stories told.
From chaos born, we rise anew,
The heart of the storm, strong and true.

In life's tempest, lessons learned,
Through trials faced, our spirits burned.
Together we stand, in trust, we form,
The eye of the storm, a healing warm.

Echoes in the Silence

In the still of night, whispers flow,
Carried on winds, soft and slow.
Memories linger, shadows play,
Echoes of love, forever stay.

Stars above, they gently gleam,
Guiding the lost with silver beams.
In the absence, hearts may find,
Tender moments left behind.

Footsteps echo on the ground,
Search for peace, yet none is found.
Silence speaks in volumes clear,
All that's felt, forever near.

Time unfolds like petals wide,
A dance of hope, a wave, a tide.
Through the quiet, voices rise,
In this stillness, past complies.

So let the night embrace the day,
Where echoes whisper, shadows sway.
In the silence, truth is brave,
Lifes' sweet verses, hearts will save.

Flickering Lanterns

In the twilight, lanterns shine,
Flickering flames, a dance divine.
Guiding travelers, lost in night,
Bringing warmth, a gentle light.

Every glow tells a tale,
Of dreams and hopes that never pale.
Through the dark, a path is shown,
Where the heart can feel at home.

With each flicker, secrets kept,
Promises made and joys wept.
In the silence, whispers sway,
Lighting up the shadowed way.

The lanterns sway in evening's breath,
Chasing fears and thoughts of death.
Each small flame a soul's refrain,
Flickering soft through joy and pain.

By their hue, we find our way,
Through the night to greet the day.
Flickering lanterns, gleaming bright,
Guide us home through endless night.

Growing from Ashes

From the ashes, life will rise,
New blooms open, touch the skies.
Through the fire, strength is born,
In the darkness, hope adorns.

Every scar tells a story true,
Of battles fought, and visions new.
With each heartbeat, courage grows,
In the silence, resilience flows.

Like a phoenix, bright and bold,
Rising high from nights so cold.
In the struggle, grace unfolds,
Strength in spirit, fierce and bold.

Roots dig deep into the ground,
Embracing life, where peace is found.
From the ruins, dreams take flight,
Growing stronger, seeking light.

So let the ashes pave the way,
For vibrant blooms in bright array.
In the garden, life will thrive,
From the darkness, we revive.

The Infinite Path

On the journey, roads unwind,
Endless trails where dreams align.
Footsteps carried by the breeze,
Whispers soft, nature's keys.

With each turn, the world expands,
Stories woven through the lands.
Fires glow and rivers flow,
Guiding hearts where wonders grow.

In the distance, mountains rise,
Touching clouds, brushing skies.
Path of wisdom, path of grace,
Finding self in every place.

Through the seasons, time will bend,
Every journey finds its end.
Yet in the heart, the path remains,
Endless echoes, love entails.

So take the step, embrace the way,
With open heart, don't dismay.
For on this path, we're never lost,
Life's great journey is the cost.

Mending the Fragments

Shattered pieces on the floor,
A heart once whole, now sore.
With gentle hands, I start to weave,
Restoring strength, I dare believe.

Time will heal, the cracks will mend,
Each fragment tells a tale, my friend.
With patience, hope is born anew,
A canvas bright with every hue.

In shadows deep, light breaks through,
With every stitch, a promise true.
I gather shards and breathe them life,
Transforming pain, transcending strife.

Love surrounds, a quilt of grace,
In each embrace, I find my place.
The fragments talk, their voices sing,
Together now, they bring new spring.

A Tapestry of Dreams

Woven threads of hopes and fears,
Each color bright, a story nears.
In twilight hours, the visions glow,
Whispers of fate in the soft wind blow.

Stars align in velvet skies,
Painting visions with silent cries.
Each dream a stitch, hand-crafted grace,
In this tapestry, I find my place.

Rich textures blend, a vibrant swirl,
In every scene, possibilities unfurl.
To chase the light, I take a chance,
In the dance of fate, I choose to prance.

Through tangled threads and shadowed seams,
I find my way, guided by dreams.
Every pattern leads to a shore,
Where hope abounds forevermore.

The Trail of Endless Possibilities

A path unfolds beneath my feet,
Each step a choice, each moment sweet.
With open eyes, I dare to roam,
The trail leads to my true home.

Through valleys deep and mountains high,
Underneath the vast, embracing sky.
With courage found in whispered sighs,
I find my way as each day flies.

New horizons beckon, bright and clear,
A symphony of dreams draws near.
With heart aglow, I face the dawn,
Every choice a chance to carry on.

In tangled woods, I lose my way,
Yet every turn holds light of day.
For in the heart of each lost trail,
Endless possibilities prevail.

The Heart's Compass

In silence deep, my heart does speak,
A gentle pull, a tender seek.
It guides my steps through fog and mist,
Leading me where I can't resist.

With every beat, it tells me true,
Navigating paths of light and blue.
Through storms that rage and shadows creep,
It holds the secrets I wish to keep.

A compass drawn from love and grace,
With each pulse, I find my place.
It knows the way to solace bright,
A beacon shining in darkest night.

When doubts arise and shadows fall,
I trust the whispers, I hear the call.
With courage found in love's warm glow,
The heart's compass leads me where to go.

Whispers of Hope in Shattered Light

In the dusk, shadows dance with dreams,
Soft murmurs weave through fractured seams.
Beneath the stars, a flicker shines bright,
Guiding hearts through the depth of night.

Crimson hues bleed into the sky,
Painting hope as the shadows sigh.
Each tear a story, a thread of grace,
In the quiet, we find our place.

Fractured mirrors reflect our fears,
Yet within we hold the light that cheers.
With every breath, we choose to believe,
In whispers of hope, we shall achieve.

The world may crumble, the light may fade,
Yet in our hearts, true strength is laid.
Together we rise, like the dawn's embrace,
In shattered light, we find our space.

The Resilience of Silent Wishes

In the quiet, dreams take flight,
Whispers glimmer, soft and bright.
Each wish a seed in the heart's soft ground,
Waiting for courage to be unbound.

Through the storms that seek to break,
Silent wishes, we will make.
With every challenge, we stand tall,
Building strength, we shall not fall.

Time may wane, but hopes stay clear,
In the echoes, we shed our fear.
A tapestry woven with threads of gold,
Resilient stories waiting to be told.

Reach for the stars, let your heart sing,
In stillness, the promise of spring.
Though silence may sometimes feel vast,
Resilience holds the future fast.

Echoes of Tomorrow's Promise

In the distance, a melody calls,
The promise of tomorrow, through pain it thralls.
Echoes whisper secrets of the day ahead,
A tapestry bright where dreams are spread.

With each heartbeat, a rhythm designs,
A path of light where resilience shines.
In every shadow, a new chance to grow,
The echoes of hope in the winds that blow.

As dusk gives way to the morning light,
Silent promises take their flight.
In every breath, we find the grace,
The echoes of tomorrow's warm embrace.

Let the past fade, allow love to steer,
Each moment cherished, forever dear.
With open hearts, we embrace the day,
In echoes of promise, we find our way.

Wings of Ambition Amidst the Storm

Amidst the storm, ambition takes flight,
With wings spread wide, it embraces the night.
Through thunder's roar and relentless rain,
The heart beats steady, igniting the flame.

Clouds may gather, shadows may loom,
Yet dreams dance bright, dispelling the gloom.
In tempest's grasp, we learn to soar,
With every struggle, we long for more.

Through winds of doubt, through waves of strife,
We cultivate passion, nurturing life.
With courage as guide, we chase the light,
In storms of fear, we find our might.

With each setback, resolve does bloom,
Wings of ambition, we'll break through the gloom.
In the heart of the tempest, we brightly ignite,
Embracing our journey with all of our might.

Treading on Broken Glass

With each step, the shards gleam bright,
A dance of pain, a fragile flight.
Echoes linger in the air,
Silent whispers of despair.

Memories cut, yet teach to feel,
In wounds, the heart learns how to heal.
The scars remind me I am bold,
A story living, yet untold.

Through the dark, I find my way,
Each glimmer leads me to the day.
I tread with care, but sing with grace,
In every step, I find my place.

A journey forged in fiery strife,
Broken glass reflects my life.
I rise anew, through every flaw,
In shattered dreams, I find my law.

So here I stand, reclaiming light,
With every shard, I win the fight.
Treading on glass, I learn to dance,
In the rubble, I find my chance.

A Garden in the Ruins

From wreckage blooms a silent grace,
Petals soft in a forgotten place.
Weeds once claimed what life should thrive,
Now hope bursts forth, determined, alive.

Amidst the stone, the blossoms sway,
In shadows cast, they find their way.
Each color bright, in chaos, blooms,
Resilience lives where darkness looms.

Time unwinds the threads of fate,
In every crack, a chance to create.
Life persists in the harshest ground,
In every heartbeat, joy is found.

Seeds of change are sown with care,
In the ruins, a beauty rare.
Whispers of life, in gentle breeze,
The heart of the garden aims to please.

So here we stand, amid the past,
A garden growing, large and vast.
In the ruins, life starts anew,
With every bloom, a brighter view.

Beacons of Tomorrow

In the twilight, stars emerge bright,
Dreams take shape, a guiding light.
With every hope, the night unwinds,
A canvas painted in our minds.

Each glimmer calls out to the heart,
A promise carved, a brand new start.
Through shadows deep, our spirits soar,
Beacons shine, forevermore.

Tomorrow waits with open hands,
A world of wonders, vast and grand.
Together we'll chase the dawn,
In the embrace of a hopeful yawn.

Fear may linger, but dreams ignite,
In the darkness, we find our light.
With courage stitched in every seam,
We rise to build a brighter dream.

So let us follow, side by side,
With beacons glowing, joys collide.
For in our hearts, the future glows,
A tapestry where courage flows.

Horizons Yet to Explore

Beyond the mountains, skies unfold,
A tale of journeys yet untold.
With every step, the earth invites,
The call of dreams ignites our sights.

Through valleys wide, we wander free,
In every breath, a new decree.
Curious hearts carve out the path,
As laughter dances in our wake.

Stars align on distant shores,
A map of dreams, no locked doors.
With open eyes, we chase the dawn,
A symphony where hope is drawn.

Each sunset paints the sky with grace,
A canvas vast, our sacred space.
In every heartbeat, whispers soar,
Horizons call; we seek for more.

So let us sail on seas unknown,
With every wave, our spirits grown.
For in the journey lies the key,
To worlds unseen, yet meant to be.

Fractured Wings

In quiet skies where shadows dwell,
A bird with wings, once strong, now fell.
It spreads its heart, to rise once more,
Through broken dreams, it seeks to soar.

Each feather lost, a story told,
Of battles fought, of courage bold.
Yet hope persists, it lights the way,
To mend the wings, to greet the day.

With every gust, it learns to glide,
Embracing flaws, it learns with pride.
The sky, though vast, will not confine,
For fractured wings can still align.

The whispers come, from winds above,
Reminding the heart it's still enough.
A journey long, but worth the flight,
To find the strength, to chase the light.

Resilience in the Rain

The raindrops fall like whispered dreams,
Each drop a challenge, it gently seems.
Yet roots run deep, they hold their ground,
Through storms and trials, strength is found.

The rivers swell, they rush and flow,
But seeds of hope beneath the snow.
In darkest nights, the stars align,
Resilience grows, like tangled vine.

With every clash, a heart beats strong,
In rhythm with the rain's soft song.
A dance of storms, a chance to grow,
For in the struggle, life will glow.

So let the droplets cleanse our pain,
For after storms, blooms will remain.
In puddles deep, reflections shine,
A testament to strength divine.

Threads of Ambition

A tapestry of dreams interlace,
With every choice we find our place.
Each thread a path, a chance we take,
In patterns bold, the fears we break.

The loom of life, it spins so fast,
With hopes that flicker, shadows cast.
But in our hands, we hold the fate,
To weave our story, to create.

For every struggle draws the line,
Through colors bright, our will will shine.
In quiet strength, we find the grace,
To thread the needle, find our space.

Ambition burns, a fire within,
Driving us forth, igniting the skin.
With every stitch, a brighter day,
A masterpiece on bright display.

The Canvas of Possibility

A canvas wide, with colors bold,
Each stroke a dream, a tale unfolds.
In vibrant hues, the heart draws near,
To paint the hopes, to quell the fear.

With brushes dipped in passions bright,
We sketch our visions, ignite the night.
Lines intertwine, creating form,
In every tempest, we transform.

The palette holds both light and dark,
In contrast lies the silent spark.
With every shade, new worlds we find,
In every vision, future aligned.

So splash with joy, unleash the soul,
For on this canvas, we are whole.
A masterpiece that knows no end,
In every heart, our dreams ascend.

Heartbeats of Tomorrow

In whispers soft, the future calls,
A gentle pulse that never stalls.
With every beat, the dreams arise,
A tapestry beneath the skies.

Seeds of hope in gardens sown,
Through trials faced, we have grown.
In shadows deep, our strength revealed,
A brighter sun, our fate is sealed.

Moments fleeting, yet they stay,
Guiding us along the way.
A chorus sung in hearts we hold,
Echoes sweet, a tale retold.

With every tear we've had to share,
A bond that forms, a love laid bare.
Through time and space, we chase the light,
A dance of joy, we take our flight.

So let us walk where dreams reside,
In heartbeats strong, we will confide.
Together bound, we face the fight,
With every dawn, we claim our right.

The Promise of Dawn

As night retreats, the stars take flight,
A promise lies in morning light.
With hues of gold, the sky does bloom,
Awakening dreams that cast out gloom.

The world anew, with colors bright,
Transformation in each ray of light.
In every shadow, hope will gleam,
A whispered vow, a waking dream.

The birds take wing, their songs set free,
A symphony of possibility.
In every heartbeat, stories weave,
With each new day, we dare believe.

Time flows gently, a river wide,
In its embrace, our fears collide.
Yet with each dawn, we start afresh,
In every breath, we find our flesh.

Together we rise, hand in hand,
In the promise, we firmly stand.
With dreams ignited, we will soar,
To the horizon, forevermore.

Singed Pages Turning

In fires of life, our stories burn,
With ink of dreams, we twist and turn.
Each page a scar, each word a fight,
A testament to our restless night.

Memories dance like shadows past,
In pages worn, our hearts are cast.
The tales unfold beneath the ash,
In flickers of hope, our spirits clash.

Through trials faced, the ink may smudge,
Yet wisdom gains, as we won't budge.
Each singed corner speaks of time,
In lessons learned, we find our rhyme.

With every flip, the future calls,
A testament where courage sprawls.
In every chapter, we reclaim,
A fiery heart that knows no shame.

So let us write with passion fierce,
In ink that won't the past disperse.
For in our stories, lives intertwine,
With singed pages, our souls align.

The Resilient Flame

In darkest nights, a spark remains,
A flicker bright, amidst the chains.
The winds may howl, the storms may roar,
Yet in our hearts, the flame will soar.

With courage fierce, we stand our ground,
In embers warm, our strength is found.
Through trials faced, we will not yield,
For in this battle, love's our shield.

As shadows creep, we hold our light,
In every step, we claim our right.
The passion burns, a guiding star,
In unity, we've come so far.

In every flame, a story lives,
A testament of what love gives.
Through every struggle, we will thrive,
In shared belief, we shall survive.

So here we stand, forever bold,
In the resilient flame, our hearts unfold.
With every breath, we'll ever burn,
In hope unleashed, we shall return.

Notes of a Wounded Bird

Upon the branch, she weeps in sighs,
With tattered wings, beneath the skies.
A song of loss, yet still she tries,
To reach the sun, where hope now lies.

In silence deep, her heart does mend,
With every note, she seeks to blend.
A melody for what might end,
A whispered prayer, a gentle trend.

The world below moves fast, it seems,
While she reflects on faded dreams.
Through open skies, her spirit beams,
In every hush, a feathered theme.

Though shadows loom and doubts arise,
She learns to dance in gray replies.
With every flap, her courage flies,
The song of life beneath the skies.

A wounded bird, yet bold and free,
In every note, her history.
Through trials faced, she finds decree,
In the symphony of what can be.

In the Wake of Disasters

The winds howl loud, the skies turn gray,
What once was whole now falls away.
In trembling hearts, the shadows play,
As hope retreats, and fears hold sway.

Among the ruins, whispers rise,
Stories of pain, beneath the skies.
Yet in the wreckage, something lies,
A spark of strength, that never dies.

In shattered dreams, new paths are made,
As life reclaims what fear had frayed.
Through tearful nights, the dawn's cascade,
Brings forth the light, the heart's parade.

Resilience blooms where chaos breathes,
Among the lost, the soul believes.
In every crack, a plan weaves,
From ashes cold, a spirit cleaves.

The storm may rage, but we endure,
With every tear, we find a cure.
In unity, our hearts are pure,
Together strong, we shall ensure.

The Soul's Odyssey

In restless waves, the journey starts,
With open eyes and trembling hearts.
Through tangled paths, where silence parts,
The soul embarks, its longing sparks.

In lands unknown, where shadows creep,
A quest unfolds, its truths to reap.
With every rhythm, secrets seep,
In whispered dreams, our fears run deep.

The skies may shift, the storms may rise,
Yet in each trial, wisdom lies.
With every step, our spirits prize,
The light that dances in our eyes.

Through valleys low and mountains steep,
The echoes call, like memories keep.
In every choice, the heart must leap,
A journey vast, its wonders heap.

In every story, threads entwine,
Our souls connect, a sacred sign.
Through every loss, a bridge divine,
In the odyssey, our hearts align.

The Flame that Endures

In darkest night, a flicker glows,
A gentle warmth, as courage grows.
Against the odds, the spirit knows,
The flame that fights, through trials flows.

With every gust, it bends but stays,
A beacon bright amidst the haze.
In tender moments, love displays,
The strength that lights our wavering ways.

When shadows fall, and doubts arise,
A steady flame beneath the skies.
In whispered prayers, our hopes comply,
As hearts unite, and fears subside.

Through storms of grief and waves of pain,
The fire persists, a fierce refrain.
In unity, we break the chain,
To fan the flame, in joy, in strain.

The flame that endures, a sacred call,
In every heart, it conquers all.
Through whispered dreams and shadows tall,
It lights the way, it never falls.

The Journey of a Thousand Before

Step by step upon this road,
With shadows of the past we strode.
In every heart, a fire glows,
A story etched where wisdom flows.

Across the hills, the echoes call,
Through every rise and every fall.
The dreams we chase, the paths we take,
In unity, our spirits wake.

With open arms, the world invites,
To dance with joy on starlit nights.
Each lesson learned, a hope renewed,
In every heart, compassion viewed.

With burdens shared, we stand as one,
Embracing rays of morning sun.
Our journey vast, yet hearts align,
In every step, a trace divine.

So onward forth with courage bright,
Through darkest paths, we seek the light.
The journey's long, but never alone,
In every stride, our strength has grown.

Dawn after the Longest Night

In quiet hours, the shadows fade,
A whisper soft, the night betrayed.
With golden hues, the sky ignites,
Embracing hope, the dawn invites.

The world awakens, dreams take flight,
As stars retreat, lost to the light.
Each dew-kissed blade, a promise made,
In every heart, dawn's glow displayed.

Through trials faced and fears let go,
A canvas bright, with colors glow.
With every breath, the past dissolves,
In light's embrace, the soul resolves.

With open skies, we chase the day,
Leaving behind what led us astray.
Together we'll rise, as shadows flee,
In every moment, we are free.

The longest night has come to rest,
In tender light, our hearts are blessed.
With every dawn, new dreams are drawn,
A symphony of hope reborn.

Seeds of Tomorrow in Stormy Weather

In tempest's grip, the world may shake,
Yet in the soil, the seeds we make.
Through rain and wind, they push and strive,
In darkest hours, they will survive.

Each drop that falls, a tale unfolds,
Of dreams entwined, through strife, they hold.
With roots so deep, they seek the sun,
In trials faced, new life begun.

Though storms may rage and shadows loom,
In hearts of clay, we find our bloom.
For every challenge, a chance to grow,
In every struggle, strength we know.

As skies clear up, a brighter hue,
The buds emerge, adorned with dew.
With petals spread, the world shall see,
The beauty forged in adversity.

For every seed, a story waits,
Of hope and dreams in stormy fates.
Together we'll rise, both strong and free,
In the garden of tomorrow, we'll be.

When Stars Align through the Gloom

In shadowed nights, the stars remain,
A beacon bright through endless pain.
With whispered light, they guide the way,
In darkest times, they softly sway.

Each twinkle holds a tale untold,
Of love and warmth through winters cold.
When dreams seem lost, they spark the fire,
A flicker of hope, a fierce desire.

Through tangled paths and winding roads,
We walk together, share the loads.
With hearts entwined, we make our stand,
In unity, we understand.

As constellations weave their song,
A promise held, we all belong.
For even in the looming night,
The stars align to share their light.

So trust the journey, hand in hand,
For brighter days will soon expand.
When stars align against the gloom,
New worlds arise from dreams in bloom.

Whispers of Hope

In the stillness of night, a dream may bloom,
A gentle sigh that chases away gloom.
Softly it calls, the heart to embrace,
Whispers of hope in a quiet space.

Stars flicker above, with stories untold,
In their glow, brave souls are bold.
Through the dark, a light will ignite,
Guiding the lost towards the bright.

When the dawn breaks, fears start to fade,
With every step, new paths are made.
Hope dances lightly on morning's breath,
A promise of life, defying death.

Together we stand, with hands entwined,
Through storms and trials, our hearts aligned.
With whispers of hope, we'll rise anew,
For every ending brings visions true.

So let us cherish each moment kind,
In the tapestry of life, our spirits bind.
With whispers of hope, we pave the road,
To brighter tomorrows, we'll share the load.

Shattered But Soaring

Once a heart, now a thousand shards,
Each piece reflecting battles, the scars.
But beneath the weight of every ache,
A spirit rises, unyielding and awake.

Fragments of dreams, tossed on the floor,
Each shard a tale of what came before.
Yet soaring high, like a phoenix in flight,
We gather the pieces and chase the light.

With every fall, we learn to climb,
Embracing the chaos, through space and time.
Though shattered and worn, we find our way,
With courage as fuel, we greet the day.

For from the ashes, new visions grow,
A tapestry woven, with colors aglow.
Shattered we are, but our spirits fly,
Unbound by the past, we reach for the sky.

So let the world see our scars with pride,
For in every darkness, a light will abide.
Shattered but soaring, we'll dance with grace,
Crafting a future, our own sacred space.

The Light Beyond Shadows

In the realm where shadows softly play,
A flicker of light begins to sway.
It whispers secrets only brave hearts know,
Guiding the way where dreams can grow.

Through depths of despair, the soul will seek,
To find the shimmer where hope is meek.
Beyond the veil, where darkness hides,
The light beckons, as fear subides.

With every heartbeat, a brightness ignites,
Illuminating paths and starry nights.
In the silence, the truth appears,
The light beyond shadows calms our fears.

Together we wander, hand in hand,
Across the hills and through the sand.
We'll chase the glow, undaunted and free,
For the light beyond shadows is our decree.

Through valleys deep and mountains high,
We'll rise as one, reaching for the sky.
The light beyond shadows, our guiding star,
Together we'll soar, no matter how far.

Echoes of Tomorrow

In the whispering winds, future calls,
With echoes of dreams that softly fall.
Each promise carried on fleeting breath,
Hints of love that transcends death.

Time travels swiftly, a river flows,
Where moments linger, the heart knows.
Every laugh, every tear that we send,
Leaves ripples behind, around the bend.

With every sunrise, the past finds grace,
In the tapestry woven, it finds its place.
Echoes of laughter, of love and pride,
Tomorrow's hope, in hearts it resides.

So hold on tightly to what feels true,
In the dance of life, make every move.
For echoes of tomorrow remain profound,
In memories cherished, where love is found.

With dreams unending, we'll stitch the seams,
Of future visions and cherished dreams.
Echoes of tomorrow, a symphony clear,
Together we'll weave what we hold dear.

The Heart's Compass Towards Infinity

In the quiet of the night, stars align,
Whispers of dreams begin to unwind.
Guiding the soul through shadows and light,
The heart's compass draws paths so divine.

Winds of change stir the leaves on the tree,
Each gust a promise, a beckoning plea.
Chasing horizons where hope finds its form,
Together we weather the calm and the storm.

With every step, the journey unfolds,
Stories of courage from hearts made of gold.
The universe stretches, vast and profound,
In the dance of existence, our truth can be found.

Lost in the moment, yet chasing the years,
Facing the dawn through laughter and tears.
Love is the anchor when tides try to shift,
Together we sail, our spirits adrift.

As time weaves its fabric, each thread a pearl,
Fingers entwined, in the vastness we twirl.
In the heart's compass, infinity glows,
Guided by love, where the wild river flows.

Blooming in the Cracks of Solidity

Through concrete jungles, a flower breaks free,
Colorful petals dance with empathy.
Resilience whispers in every bold hue,
A testament, beauty finds ways to renew.

In the heart of despair, hope finds its light,
Growing in shadows, embracing the night.
Amidst the harshness, a softness can thrive,
Life springs eternal, where dreams come alive.

Amongst the rubble, a story unfolds,
Daring the darkness, a spirit so bold.
Roots buried deeply, yet reaching for skies,
In every struggle, a chance to arise.

Seeking the sun, through resilience we soar,
From cracks of solidity, we bloom evermore.
Nature's sweet magic, a lesson of grace,
In the hardest of places, we find our place.

So cherish each petal, each blossom that grows,
From stubborn foundations, the beauty still shows.
In the cracks of our lives, where light softly seeps,
Lies a garden of dreams, where the heart truly leaps.

The Melody of a Fading Echo

In twilight's embrace, a whisper takes flight,
Songs of tomorrow blend soft with the night.
Echoes of laughter, like ripples in time,
Fade into stillness, a soft, haunting rhyme.

Memories linger, like shadows at dusk,
Fragile and fleeting, they stir as we trust.
In silence, we hear the melodies call,
A dance of the past, where shadows might fall.

Lost in the music, a heart finds its tune,
In the cracks of the night, under the moon.
Melodies weaving through stories untold,
Each note a treasure, a memory held.

Though echoes may wane, their essence remains,
In corridors of heart, love's quiet refrains.
A tapestry woven with threads of the past,
The melody lingers, though moments may pass.

So listen intently, for echoes still play,
In the quiet of night, they guide us each day.
In every soft whisper, a promise, a spark,
The melody lingers, illuminating the dark.

Beyond the Horizon of Lost Chances

At the edge of dawn, where dreams gently weave,
Lies a horizon where hearts dare believe.
Echoes of wishes escape with the tide,
Whispers of moments where courage must stride.

In the shadows of doubt, we gather our fears,
Counting the chances through laughter and tears.
Each heartbeat a promise, a tale yet to spin,
Beyond all the losses, new journeys begin.

The sun breaks the silence, painting the skies,
With colors of hope, as the past softly sighs.
Every setback a lesson, each stumble a chance,
In the dance of resilience, we learn to advance.

So take a deep breath, embrace what will be,
In the tapestry woven, find strength to be free.
Beyond the horizon, where lost chances gleam,
Awaits a tomorrow, alive with the dream.

With open hearts ready, we venture ahead,
For hope is a song that's eternally said.
Beyond all the shadows, a light softly glows,
In the vastness of time, our spirit still flows.

Stars Still Shine

In the quiet of the night,
Stars awaken to the light.
Whispers of dreams take flight,
Guiding hearts through sheer delight.

Glimmers twinkle from afar,
Each a promise, each a star.
Hope ignites in every soul,
Knowing love will make us whole.

Underneath the endless sky,
Wishes lift and softly sigh.
In the dark, we find our way,
Chasing shadows into day.

Radiant beams, a cosmic dance,
Inviting eyes to take a chance.
Hold tight to the gleaming glow,
For in their light, we come to know.

Stars will guide us, softly bright,
Through the depths and darkest night.
In their glow, our spirits rise,
Forever bound to starry skies.

Beyond the Veil of Night

In the silence of the dark,
Whispers dance, a gentle spark.
Dreams unfold like fragile lace,
Time stands still, a sacred space.

Shadows weave their secret tales,
While the moon glows, calm prevails.
Stars emerge, a guiding hand,
Leading us to undisclosed lands.

Heartbeats echo through the void,
In the stillness, fears destroyed.
Beyond the veil, where hopes ignite,
We find courage with the night.

Each breath carries a soft plea,
To embrace what's yet to be.
Open eyes to truth unveiled,
In the darkness, dreams are hailed.

Journey forth with open mind,
In the quiet, answers find.
Trust the night, its gentle call,
For beyond the veil lies it all.

Boundless Horizons

Across the fields, the endless sky,
Where dreams are born and spirits fly.
Mountains rise and rivers flow,
In this vast world, let passions grow.

Footsteps trace the paths untold,
Every journey, brave and bold.
Under sun or silver moon,
Hearts entwined, we'll find our tune.

Waves crash upon the golden shore,
Echoes of life, forevermore.
In the distance, new worlds call,
Chasing dreams, we'll never fall.

Adventure waits beyond each bend,
With every moment, we ascend.
Open arms to what life brings,
In boundless horizons, our heart sings.

With courage stoked by embers bright,
We'll embrace the morning light.
Together, we shall ride the tide,
In every moment, love our guide.

Through the Cracks of Despair

In shadows deep, where silence lingers,
Hope peeks through with tender fingers.
A whispered breath, a soft refrain,
Reminds us joy can rise from pain.

Cracks of sorrow, paths unknown,
Yet through the dark, seeds are sown.
In the struggle, strength is found,
Emerging flames from ashes crowned.

Every tear, a step toward grace,
Through the trials, we find our place.
In heartache's grip, we learn to fight,
Turning darkness into light.

So when despair feels like the end,
Lift your gaze, let hope ascend.
For through the cracks, the sun will shine,
Revealing love's pure, endless line.

Hold tight to dreams, let fears dissolve,
In time, our troubles will resolve.
Through the cracks, we'll find our way,
Into the dawn of a new day.

Phoenix Rising

From ashes deep, a spark ignites,
A tale of strength in endless nights.
With wings outstretched, I soar anew,
The flames have shaped a heart so true.

In vibrant colors, hope alights,
A beacon shining through the flights.
Each trial faced, a lesson learned,
From every fall, a fire returned.

No shadows cast can hold me down,
In courage found, I wear my crown.
The past transforms, a canvas bright,
As I embrace my inner light.

With every gust that dares to blow,
I rise above the undertow.
With every moment, I reclaim,
This new existence, fierce and tame.

So let the winds of change ascend,
In strength I find, the will to mend.
A spirit born, forever free,
I stand as one, the phoenix me.

The Dance of Recovery

In gentle steps, the journey starts,
With weary souls and hopeful hearts.
Each movement swift, a chance to heal,
In rhythm found, the wounds conceal.

A melody of grace unfolds,
In whispers soft, the strength it holds.
The shadows fade, the light draws near,
As bodies sway, we shed our fear.

Through trials deep, we learn to stand,
With open hearts and joined hands.
A dance of joy, a world reborn,
In every step, a new hope sworn.

With every twirl, a spirit buys,
A fleeting glance at brighter skies.
The rhythm pulses, strong and clear,
A symphony of life's frontier.

United now, we find our place,
In every heartbeat, shared embrace.
Together we shall face the fight,
In dance, we find the will to light.

Emblems of Strength

Each scar I wear, a story told,
Of battles fought, and courage bold.
In quiet strength, I forge my way,
The past a guide, I won't betray.

Emblems worn, they speak of grace,
In trials faced, I've found my space.
With every step, my heart beats strong,
In unity, I know I belong.

The weight I carry, not alone,
In every struggle, resilience grown.
The echoes of the past remind,
In every shadow, light I find.

With open arms, I greet the dawn,
A new day breaks, the night is gone.
These symbols true, my guiding star,
In every challenge, I've come so far.

Together, we are never weak,
In every voice, strength starts to speak.
Emblems of courage, here we rise,
In unity, we touch the skies.

A Journey Reclaimed

Pathways worn, but never lost,
Through every storm, I count the cost.
With every step, I learn to see,
The essence of who I can be.

In whispers soft, the voices call,
Through ups and downs, I've faced it all.
Each moment cherished, lessons gained,
Through trials faced, my heart unchained.

A tapestry of dreams unfolds,
With threads of courage, brightly bold.
The journey long, but worth the strife,
With every breath, I reclaim life.

The winding road, a sacred guide,
In every turn, new hope resides.
Through shadows cast, the light breaks through,
In gratitude, I make it true.

A journey clear, the future bright,
In every step, I claim my light.
With open arms, I face the day,
Together we'll find a brighter way.

The Symmetry of Hope

In the quiet dawn, dreams start to bloom,
Gentle whispers scatter away the gloom.
Each ray of light, a promise held tight,
Dancing shadows weave through day and night.

Beneath the surface, strength starts to rise,
Resilient hearts find solace in the skies.
With every heartbeat, a story unfolds,
Hope like a phoenix, fiercely bold.

In the darkest hours, a flicker remains,
Winds carry whispers, washing away strains.
With arms open wide, we embrace the chance,
To twirl in the light, to dream and to dance.

A bridge of trust we build without fear,
Each leap of faith brings our vision near.
Together we stand, hand in hand we cope,
Creating a future wrapped in hope.

So let us paint our lives with bright hues,
Crafting a tale of joy, we choose.
In the symmetry of love, we find our way,
And in shared dreams, forever we stay.

Veins of Inspiration

In quiet corners, ideas ignite,
Flickering candles in the still of night.
A pulse of rhythm moves through the air,
Veins of inspiration are everywhere.

Each stroke of pen, a journey begins,
The universe whispers, each secret spins.
Threads of thought, like constellations,
Connecting souls in endless creations.

With echoes of laughter that dance in our minds,
We seek the truth that our heart unwinds.
In the tapestry woven with words of light,
Dreams intertwine, bold and bright.

The heart beats softly, a soft serenade,
Within its depths, all doubts will fade.
In every heartbeat, visions ignite,
Guiding us forward on paths of delight.

Through valleys of shadow, we rise and aspire,
Fueled by the flames of our inner fire.
In veins of inspiration, we find our start,
With hope and passion, we share our art.

The Heart's Resurgence

When silence prevails, and shadows are long,
The heart begins stirring, ready to song.
With gentle whispers, it claims the light,
And rises anew, reclaiming its might.

Each scar tells a tale, of battles fought,
In the dance of the brave, resilience is sought.
Breath by breath, the spirit evolves,
In the echo of love, all mystery resolves.

In the warmth of embrace, a refuge we find,
The fortress of home, where souls are entwined.
Every throb of existence, a pulse of delight,
A testament bold to our will to ignite.

Awakening dreams that were long out of sight,
Flickers of courage burn fiercely bright.
With open hearts, we rise from despair,
In the heart's resurgence, we conquer the air.

Together we weave, with threads made of grace,
Creating our future, we find our place.
In the deepest caverns, love will prevail,
The heart's resurgence, a timeless tale.

On the Edge of Infinity

Here at the brink, where time seems to pause,
Life opens its arms, without any cause.
Endless horizons stretch out before,
Inviting us in, through an uncharted door.

Stars wink above in the vastness we seek,
Whispers of ages in every heart's beat.
As the universe dances, we step in tune,
Caught in the magic beneath the same moon.

With every heartbeat, the moment expands,
We grasp at the threads, spinning through our hands.
On this edge, we feel time's gentle sway,
Daring to dream of a brand new day.

In the fabric of space, all stories align,
A tapestry woven with love and design.
On the edge of infinity, fears disappear,
With courage in hearts, we vanish the drear.

Here at the cusp where all worlds collide,
Boundless potential, we take in our stride.
So let us leap forward, spirit unchained,
On the edge of infinity, joy is unfeigned.

www.ingramcontent.com/pod-product-compliance
Ingram Content Group UK Ltd.
Pitfield, Milton Keynes, MK11 3LW, UK
UKHW030916221224
452712UK00008B/1181